A Life for A Life and Other Addresses

A Life for A Life and Other Addresses
By Henry Drummond

Start Publishing PD LLC
Copyright © 2024 by Start Publishing PD LLC

All rights reserved, including the right to reproduce this book or portions thereof in any form whatsoever.

Start Publishing PD is a registered trademark of Start Publishing PD LLC
Manufactured in the United States of America

Cover art: Shutterstock/Taisiya Kozorez

Cover design: Jennifer Do

10 9 8 7 6 5 4 3 2 1

ISBN 979-8-8809-0036-7

Table of Contents

A Tribute . . . .
A Life for a Life . . . .
Lessons from the Angelus . . . .
The Ideal Man . . . .

A Tribute

It sometimes happens that a man, in giving to the world the truths that have most influenced his life, unconsciously writes the truest kind of a character sketch. This was so in the case of Henry Drummond, and no words of mine can better describe his life or character than those in which he has presented to us, "The Greatest Thing in the World." Some men take an occasional journey into the thirteenth of 1 Corinthians, but Henry Drummond was a man who lived there constantly, appropriating its blessings and exemplifying its teachings. As you read what he terms the analysis of love, you find that all its ingredients were interwoven into his daily life, making him one of the most lovable men I have ever known. Was it courtesy you looked for, he was a perfect gentleman. Was it kindness, he was always preferring another. Was it humility, he was simple and not courting favor. It could be said of him truthfully, as it was said of the early apostles, "that men took knowledge of him, that he had been with Jesus."

Nor was this love and kindness only shown to those who were close friends. His face was an index to his inner life. It was genial and kind, and made him, like his Master, a favorite with children. He could be the profound philosopher or the learned theologian, but I know that he preferred to be the simple friend of children and youth. Never have I known a man who, in my opinion, lived nearer the Master or sought to do His will more fully.

I well remember our first meeting in Edinburgh twenty-four years ago. He was still a divinity student in the university, but he generously gave himself to aiding me in every possible way. There was nothing that he would not undertake to do to help spread the evangelistic work among his friends in the university, and, later on, he began special meetings for young men in various towns in Great Britain. The friendship then begun has been strengthened ever since, not only by his lovable nature, but by the great blessing God has used him to be in my own life.

Never have I heard Henry Drummond utter one unkind or harsh word of criticism against any one. He was a man who was filled with love to his fellow men, because he knew by experience something of the love of Christ. He was one of the easiest men with whom to work, for he thought more of the common object than of aught else.

The news of his death has brought a sense of the deepest loss to all his friends in every part of the world. He was a man greatly beloved, and my own feelings are akin to those of David on the death of Jonathan. But although the life on earth is ended, God has called His servant higher to a sphere of greater usefulness. And when at last we meet again before our Lord and Master Jesus Christ, whom we both loved and served together in years gone, we shall no longer "see through a glass darkly; but then face to face;" and things which we could not see alike here below we shall fully know in the light of His countenances who brought our lives together and blessed them with a mutual love.

D. L. MOODY.

The following addresses were delivered at the Students' Conference in Northfield, 1893. They are now issued in permanent form for the first time.

A Life for a Life

The report to the Italian government describing a great shipwreck said, "A large ship was seen coming close to shore last night; we endeavored to give every assistance through the speaking trumpet, nevertheless four hundred and one bodies were washed ashore this morning." That shows the futility of attempting to save men by speech. It isn't the whole truth, but it is a part of the truth. In saving men it is very often a life for a life; you have to give your life to the men whom you are trying to better. About the least Christian act a man can do for his brother-man is to talk about Christianity; the case is of a man laying down his life as Christ laid down His life. Don't misunderstand me. I have an idea that some of you don't understand me: it is my fault, and I will tell you why. Because for the last three or four years of my life I have had very little to do with the ninety and nine: I have been after the one sheep that was lost, and I have got into the way of talking to that one and trying to make things plain to him. In most cases he has been a man who wouldn't accept the Bible to start with, and I have had to translate the Bible into words which he would accept, and therefore some of you don't recognize the old truth in the language of the street. If you want to get hold of an agnostic, or a man who doesn't start off by standing on the common ground with you of believing the Bible, let me ask you to try to translate what you have to say into the simplest words, into words which will not be in every case the words in which you ordinarily clothe your thought. Now while it is no more cant to talk about religion in the language of the Bible than it is cant to talk about Science in the words of Science—for religion has technical terms just as much as science has—yet it will be useful to the man who calls all that cant, and it will prove an exceedingly valuable discipline for oneself to take an old text that has been lingering in one's mind from childhood and say, "What does this really mean in nineteenth century speech?" You will find that an effort to go to the bottom of that text will give you a new grasp of it, and, that in so doing you have learned an exceedingly valuable lesson, that it doesn't matter into what phrase or words truth is put, so long as it is true.

I had an egg for breakfast this morning, and I saw that it was an egg; there it was, shell and all. God made that egg. I had an egg for dinner to-day, but it was in the pudding, and it didn't look in the least like an egg, but it did me just as much good as the egg which I had for breakfast and which I saw with my eyes. You get a ray of truth through a book, or a man, or a picture, or a tree, or the sky; it doesn't matter the form of it if it does you good, if it inspires you and draws you near to God. Don't be suspicious of it if it is God's truth, even if its form changes. In talking to a man,—if you are to win him in that way,—talk in the man's own language if you can. But I was going to say more particularly that one has to do a great deal more to display and live out his Christianity than merely to talk to people about religion. Have you ever tried to get at the real secret of what Christianity is? It isn't picking out a man here, and a man there and having them made fit to go to Heaven; Christ came into this world, as He himself said, to found a society. Have you ever thought of that conception of Christianity? For hundreds of years that conception of Christianity has been utterly lost sight of; it is only lately that men are getting back to see the great Christian doctrine of the kingdom of God. The great phrase that was never off Christ's lips was the "kingdom of God." It is by far the commonest phrase in his teaching. Have you ever given a month of your life to finding out what Christ meant by the kingdom of God? Every day as we have prayed, "Thy kingdom come," has our Christian consciousness taken in the tremendous sweep of that prayer and seen how it covers the length and breadth of this great world and every interest of human life? Christ was continually asking people to join his kingdom, and in order to get them to join it and to make no mistake about its meaning, he was continually telling them what it was: the kingdom of Heaven is like unto this, the kingdom of Heaven is like unto that; if there is one thing more common in Christ's teaching than another, it is His explanation of what the kingdom of God is, and what the subjects of that kingdom are to busy themselves in doing. Now the kingdom of God is a society of the best men, working for the best ends, with the highest motives, according to the best principles. The kingdom of God was to give them observation. Christ likened the kingdom of God to leaven, and one cannot get a better understanding of the meaning of this phrase than by taking His own metaphor. Christ saw that the world was sunken and that it had to be raised. Leaven comes from the same word as lever does, that which lifts or raises, and Christ founded a Society of men for the purpose of raising the world. The kingdom of God is like leaven. When you put leaven into a vessel with the thing which is to be leavened, it does not affect the outward form; and when leaven comes into a society, or into a church, or into a movement, or into a country, its first purpose is not to affect the outward form, but to lift the external form by changing the inward spirit of it. The kingdom of Heaven is like leaven: it is to raise men by the contact of one life with another. Did you ever put a little leaven under a microscope? If you did you found that it was a plant, perhaps six one-thousandths of an inch in diameter, with an amazing power of propagation; and that leaven simply by being in contact with the dough has the effect of lifting by means of the life that is in it; and the Christian man, simply by virtue of the life that is in him,—not by attempting much in the way of forcing it upon others,—but by his own spontaneous nature can so work upon men that they cannot but feel that he has been with Jesus. When they look through him and perceive the fragrance of his spirit and the Christlikeness of his life, they remember Christ,—they are reminded of Christ by him; and a longing comes over them to live like that, and breathe that air and have that calm, that meekness and that beauty of character; and by that unconscious influence going out as a contagious power, men are won to Christ, and by these men the world is raised. But that is not all.

The world is not only sunken; the world is rotten. Those of you who know life even an inch below the surface know that even in this Christian country, in our great cities the world is rotten. I have you ever thought of the sin of the world? Think of the sin in your own being; think that the man in the next house to you has the same amount of sin in him, and that all the people in your street are like that. Multiply that by all the streets in your city, that city by all the cities in your country, go around the world and add to that all the sin that is in all the streets in all the cities in the world, and you conjure up a ghastly spectre before which your imagination quails, and that is only a single glimpse of the sin of the world. But it can be taken away, it can be taken away: "Behold the Lamb of God who taketh away the sin of the world." How does he do it? On the cross by forgiving the sin of t he world; that is one part of it, and through you and through me and through the subjects of his kingdom. Christ said that the followers of Him are the salt of the earth and it is that salt that helps to take away the rottenness of the world. God takes away the guilt of it, and you help him to remove it by being the salt in the society in which you live. Salt is that which keeps things from becoming rotten. You put salt upon meat and salt upon fish to prevent them from becoming rotten, and it is the Christian men and women in the city and in the country who prevent them from becoming absolutely rotten. Christianity is the great antiseptic of society, and if you take the Christianity out of New York, out of Chicago, out of Berlin, or out of Paris, those cities must go to pieces. In a few generations they would go to pieces even physically by the mere accumulation of their rottenness. Now we are to be the salt of New York and of Chicago and of all the great cities of America, and it is our business to make and to keep these cities sweet, not only to sweep away the rottenness, but to prevent the new generation that is growing up from becoming rotten. The work of salt is preventative as well as curative. We do not half enough emphasize the preventative side of Christian activity; we do not half enough emphasize the making of Christian environment, in which the Christ life shall be possible even in the slums of our great cities. That man is doing the work of Christ who is cleansing these places by building new houses, by giving pure air and pure water, by giving good schools, and by in any way bringing sweetness and light and purity to keep young lives from succumbing to the influences which surround them.

That is not all. The world which you and I have to help to lift up is not only the world of the poor, but we have to lift up our whole country. One thing that strikes a stranger very much in coming to this country is this: He comes to a city like Boston, and he finds the merchants of that city with their heads buried in their ledgers, while a few Irishmen carry on the city government. I do not object to an Irishman, but it is matter in the wrong place when a company of Irishmen regulate the affairs of the city of Boston. Therefore, if you are subjects of the kingdom of God, you must work to reform the world and reform your country and reform Boston and Chicago, and above all reform New York. You have been taught in school of your duties as citizens, but you are taught in this book very plainly your duties as Christian citizens. It is your duty to make these cities, and it is possible for you to do it. These cities are making the people that live in them, and unless they set examples of righteousness and honor, the people will not be righteous and honorable. In this country there is not only little honesty and honor in municipal life, but there is little belief in its possibility. In England I have never known of a member of a government or of a municipality, or of a city accepting a bribe. When I have told that to some in America, they have received it with incredulity, because the very conception of a pure government, and of honorable city and municipal authorities has been almost lost by the nation. It is your business to restore the integrity and the righteousness in the high places of this land, and let the people see examples which will be helpful to them in their Christian life. I cannot speak too strongly about that, because I know that it can be done. We have had rotten municipal government, and the Christian men of the place have taken it up, and have said, "we are determined that this shall not be," and in the old city they have put man after man into the municipal chairs simply because they were Christian men, and because they would deal with the people righteously and carry out a program of Christianity for the city, and that can be done here.

Let me tell you what happened to the work of some University men in the city of London. They went to a district in the East End, a God-forsaken, sunken place, entirely occupied for miles by working people. They took a little house and became settlers in that poor district. They gave themselves no airs of superiority; they didn't tell the people they had come to do them good; they went in there and made friends with the people. The leaven went in among the dough, and the salt went in beside that which was corrupting. The very place where the salt should not be is beside the salt; it ought to be scattered over the meat and rubbed well into it. Well, these men went to live there, and they were in no great hurry. They waited several months and came to know quite a number of the working people; they came to understand one another. These men had studied cities, and they knew about city government, and about city life, and about education, and about cleansing, and about purity. One day there came a great labor war, and the working men put their heads together and said, "Those young men up there have good heads, let's go and talk it over with them." So they did, and in a few moments those young men were the arbiters of the strike. By a single word of theirs, three or four thousand men could be kept at work, that is three or four thousand people could be kept out of want. One of these young men after a time was elected to a Board, and in a few months was the head of that Board, and could sway that district. The other edged his way to the School-board, and soon was head of the School-board. These men did not claim to be superior; they were elected kings of the common people, because the people felt their kingship. By and by there came a time when a member of Parliament was to be chosen, and these people put in one of these young men. And so they have taken possession of that city in the name of Jesus Christ, and they are gradually working and lifting and salting It is not to be done in a day,—"first the blade, then the ear, then the full corn in the ear." It is giving them observation, but the kingdom is coming in that way, and the sin of that place is being taken away by the work of these men.

Christians are the only agents God has for carrying out His purposes. Think of that! He could himself with a single breath cleanse the whole of New York or the whole of London, but he does not do it. We are members of His body, and it is by the members of His body that He carries on His work, and we all have a different piece of that work to do.

Some of us are limbs and must use our fingers, and some of us are only a little bit of a little finger, and others are brains. God is in everyone, and all are essential to the coming of His kingdom.

Now that conception of Christianity as a kingdom is beginning to go throughout Christendom at this hour. Every age has emphasized its peculiar side of Christianity, and the side that is just now being emphasized above all others is that social side, that large conception of what Christ came to do, how He came to save men, as it were, in the bulk,—by the city and by the country—and the movements that are going on just now in society, in education, in sanitation, in University Extension, in philanthropy, are all working together for good in that direction; and let us who believe in the salvation of the individual soul as the supreme thing not startle away the supreme thing. Let us not shut our eyes to the Christianity of Christ, to His great conception of the kingdom of God.

There are two functions discharged by every living being, and by every plant: one is the struggle for its own life,—the function of nutrition; the other is the struggle for the life of others,—the function of reproduction. All the activities of life may be classed under one or the other of these two heads, and all the activities of the Christian may be classed under one or the other of these two heads, the function of nutrition and the function of reproduction. You go from a Conference fairly well fed; the individual life has been attended to, now what is to become of this unless it is to go out in different ways for the helping of this universal movement for the bringing of the world to Christ. I know that many of you are puzzled to know in what direction you can start to help Christ, to help this world. Let me simply say this to you in that connection: Once I came to crossroads in the old life, and did not know in which direction God wanted me to help to hasten His kingdom. I started to read the Book to find out what the ideal life was, and I found that the only thing worth doing in the world was to do the will of God; whether that was done in the pulpit or in the slums, whether it was done in the college or class-room or on the street did not matter at all. "My meat and my drink," Christ said, "is to do the will of him that sent me," and if you make up your mind that you are going to do the will of God above everything else, it matters little in what direction you work. There are more posts waiting for men than there are men waiting for posts. Christ needs men in every community and in every land; it matters little whether we go to foreign lands or stay at home, as long as we are sure that we are where God puts us. I am not jealous of the great missionary movement which has swept this country and which has also swept ours. In my own college at least one third of the men are going to the foreign mission field. I am not jealous of that movement, I rejoice in it, but I should like also to plead for my country and for your country. Men say, "How am I to know whether I am to go there or to stay at home?" Let me give you one or two points on the subject.

The first thing of course is, Pray. I need not enlarge upon that. The only reason that a man should speak at all is because he says things that are not being said. The second thing is, Think. Think over all the different lines of work and think over all your own qualifications. If you want to go to the missionary field, think over the different kinds of missionary fields. There are some kinds of missionary fields which do not need you at all, and there may be others for which you are just the right man. It is a mistake to imagine that missionary work is all the same. The man who is going to the missionary field had better not go to his field unequipped with a knowledge of the people and the country. A third thing is, Take the advice of wise friends, but do not regard their decision as final; no other man can plan your life for you. Let me say also in that connection, do not imagine that the most disagreeable of two or three alternatives that may be before you is necessarily the will of God. God's will does not always lie in the line of the disagreeable; God likes to see His children happy just as fathers like to see their children happy, and there may be plums waiting for you as well as stones. Do not sacrifice yourself to a thing that is disagreeable unless you are quite sure that it is the will of God. The fourth is, When the time comes for decision, act, go ahead with what light you have, you will find a turn of the road somewhere. The fifth thing is, Having once decided, don't reconsider your decision. The day after a man makes a great life decision, he does not always allow himself to think he has done the right thing. If you make a decision once, let that be final. And the last thing is, That you will probably not know for months or years that you have done the right thing, but then you will see that God has led you every step of the way. One good general rule is, go in the direction of least resistance. If you have nothing positive to urge you on, and find objections to every scheme, go in the direction where there is least resistance.

I want to return again just for a moment or two to the immediate purposes of those of you who have a year or two of college life before you, and I ask you to study what Christianity is, and to spread the knowledge of that through your University. There are many in the University who do not know in the least what Christianity is. When I was in the University I thought Christianity was something you could put upon the point of a needle, and I thought that Christ was a being so small that you had to search hard for Him before you found Him, but now I know that the whole earth is full of His glory, and I know that there is no scheme that has ever been conceived by the mind of man so great as the vision of Christ when he prayed, "Thy kingdom come," and saw the nations of the earth becoming subjects of His rule. Study the kingdom of God, see what Christ said it was like, and how it was coming to be great, and how the members of that kingdom were to act, and pass it on to the other men, pass it on to the lawyers, pass it on to the doctors, until we have the professions Christianized, and the country will follow.

Begin with individuals; give your life for a life. Let me illustrate by recalling to you the case of a man whom I shall never forget to my dying day. One night I got a letter from one of the students of the University of Edinburgh, page after page of agnosticism and atheism. I went over to see him and spent a whole afternoon with him and did not make the slightest impression. At Edinburgh University, we have a Students' Evangelistic meeting Sunday nights at which there are eight hundred or one thousand men present. A few nights after this, I saw that man in the meeting, and next to him sat another man whom I had seen occasionally at the meetings, I did not know his name, but I wanted to find out more about my skeptic, so when the meeting was over, I went up to him and said, "Do you happen to know Boyce?" "Yes," he replied, "it is he that has brought me to Edinburgh." "Are you an old friend?" I asked. "I am an American, a graduate of an American University," he said. "After I had finished there I wanted to take a post-graduate course, and finally decided to come to Edinburgh. In the dissecting room I happened to be placed next to Boyce, and I took a singular liking for him. I found out that he was a man of very remarkable ability, though not a religious man, and I thought I might be able to do something for him. A year passed and he was just where I found him." He certainly was blind enough, because it was only two or three weeks before that that he wrote me that letter. "I think you said," I resumed, "that you only came here to take a year of the postgraduate course." "Well," he said, "I packed my trunks to go home, and I thought of this friend, and I wondered whether a year of my life would be better spent to go and start in my profession in America, or to stay in Edinburgh and try to win that one man for Christ, and I stayed."

Well," I said, "my dear fellow, it will pay you; you will get that man." Two or three months passed, and it came to the last night of our meetings. We have men in Edinburgh from every part of the world. Every year, five or six hundred of them go out never to meet again, and in our religious work, we get very close to one another, and on the last night of the year we sit down together in our common hall to the Lord's Supper. This is entirely a students' meeting. On that night we get in the members of the theological faculty, so that things may be done decently and in order. Hundreds of men are there, the cream of the youth of the world, sitting down at the Lord's Table. Many of them are not members of the church, but are there for the first time pledging themselves to become members of the kingdom of God. I saw Boyce sitting down and handing the communion cup to his American friend. He had got his man. A week after, he was back in his own country. I do not know his name; he made no impression in our country, nobody knew him. He was a subject of Christ's kingdom, doing His work in silence and in humility. A few weeks passed and Boyce came to see me I said, "What do you come here for?" He said, "I want to tell you I am going to be a Medical Missionary." It was worth a year, was it not?

Before you leave, gentlemen, before you leave Northfield, make up your mind that with God's help you will try and win your man. Let us try and lead souls to Christ, if He can use us in that way.

Lessons from the Angelus

Students are recommended to invest in certain books; I am going to take the liberty to suggest to you the buying of a certain picture which you can get for a very few cents; it is Millais' Angelus.

God speaks to men's souls through music, and He also speaks through art. This famous picture is an illuminated text, and upon it I want to hang what I have to say to-night.

There are three things in this picture—a potato field, a country lad and a country girl standing in the middle of it, and upon the far horizon the spire of a village church. That is all—no great scenery, and no picturesque people.

In Roman Catholic countries at the evening hour the church bell rings out to remind the people to pray. Some go into the church to pray, while those that are in the fields, when the Angelus rings, bow their heads for a few moments in silent prayer.

That picture is a perfect portraiture of the Christian life; and what is interesting about it apart from the fact that it singles out the three great pedestals upon which a symmetrical life is lived, is the completeness of the truth that it contains. I recall how often Mr. Moody has told us that it is not enough to have the roots of religion in us, but that we must be whole and entire, lacking nothing.

The Angelus, as we look upon it, will reveal to us the elements which constitute the complete life.

The first of these is work. Three-fourths of our life is probably spent in work. Is that religious or is it not? What is the meaning of it? Of course the meaning of it is that our work should be just as religious as our worship, and that unless we can make our work religious, three-fourths of life remains unsanctified.

The proof that work is religious is that the most of Christ's life was spent in work. During those first thirty years of his life, the Scriptures were not in His hands so much as the hammer and the plane; He was making chairs and tables and ploughs and yokes; which is to say that the highest conceivable life was mainly spent in doing common work. Christ's public ministry occupied only about two and a half years; the great bulk of His time He was simply at work, and ever since then work has had a new meaning.

When Christ came into the world, He came to men at their work. He appeared to the shepherds, the working classes of those days; He appeared also to the wise men, the students of those days. Three deputations went out to meet Him. First came the shepherds, second the wise men, and third the two old people, Simeon and Anna—that is to say, Christ comes to men at their work, He comes to men at their books, and He comes to men at their worship. But you will notice that it was the old people who found Christ at their worship, and as we grow older we will spend more time in worship, and will repair to the prayer meeting and the house of God to meet Christ and to worship Him as Simeon and Anna did. But until the age comes when much of our time will be given to direct vision, we must try to find Christ at our books and in our common work.

Now why should God have arranged it that so many hours of every day should be occupied with work? It is because work makes men. A University is not merely a place for making scholars, it is a place for making Christians. A farm is not a place for growing corn, it is a place for growing character, and a man has no character except what is built up through the medium of the things that he does from day to day. God's Spirit does the building through the acts which a man performs during his life work. If a student cons out every word in his latin instead of consulting a translation, the result is that honesty is translated into his character; if he works out his mathematical problems thoroughly, he not only becomes a mathematician, but a thorough man; if he attends to the instructions that are given him in the class-room intelligently and conscientiously, he becomes a conscientious man. It is just by such means that thoroughness and conscientiousness and honorableness are imbedded in our being. We cannot dream perfect character; we do not get it in our sleep; it comes to us as muscle comes, through doing things. Character is the muscle of the soul, and it is developed by the practice of the muscles, and by exercising it upon actual things; hence our work is the making of us, and it is by and through our work that the great Christian graces are communicated to our soul. That is the means which God employs for the growing of the Christian graces, and apart from that we cannot have a Christian character. Hence the religion of a student consists first of all in his being true to his work, and in letting his Christianity be shown to his fellow students and to his professors by the integrity and the thoroughness of his academic work. If he is not faithful in that which is least, it will be impossible for him to be faithful in that which is great. I have known men who struggled unsuccessfully for years to pass their examinations, who when they became Christians, found a new motive for work, and thus were able to succeed where previously they had failed.

There are men here who have much intellectual energy; if they can but see that a man's Christianity comes out as much in his work as in his worship, they will find a new motive and stimulus to do their work thoroughly. Our work is not only to be done thoroughly, it is to be done honestly. By this I mean not so much that a man must be honorable in his academic relations, as that he must be fair to his own mind, and to the principles of the truth. We are not entitled to dodge difficulties, when they arise it is our duty to go to the bottom of them. Perhaps the truths which are dear to us are deeper even than we think, and we can get more out of them if we dig down for the nuggets. Others may perhaps be found to have false bases; if so, we ought to know it.

Christianity is the most important thing in the world, and the student ought to sound it in every direction to see if there is deep water and a safe place in which to launch his life; if there are shoals he ought to know it. Therefore, when we come to difficulties, let us not be guilty of jumping lightly over them, but let us be honest as seekers after truth,—which is the definition of a student. It may not be necessary for people in general to sift the doctrines of Christianity for themselves, but it is required of a student, whose business it is to think, to exercise the intellect which God has given him in living out the truth. Faith is never opposed to reason, though it is often supposed that the Bible teaches that it is, but you will find that it is not. Faith is opposed to sight but not to reason. It is only by reason that we can sift and examine and criticise and be sure of the forms of truth which are given us as Christians. Hence the great field of work that is open to a student is in seeking for truth, and let him be sure that in seeking for truth he is drawing very near to Christ who said: "I am the way, and the truth, and the life." We talk a great deal about Christ as the Way and Christ as the Life, but there is a side of Christ especially for the student, "I am the Truth;" and every student ought to be a truth lover and a truth seeker for Christ's sake.

Another element in life which of course is first in importance, is God. The Angelus is perhaps the most religious picture painted during this century. You cannot look at it and see that young man standing in the field with his hat off and the girl opposite him with her hands clasped and her head bowed upon her breast without feeling a sense of God. Do we carry about with us a sense of God? Do we carry the thought of Him with us wherever we go? If not, we have missed the greatest part of life. Do we have that feeling and a conviction of God's abiding presence wherever we are? There is nothing more needed in this generation than a larger and more scriptural idea of God. A great American writer has told us that when he was a boy the conception of God which he got from books and sermons was that of a wise and very strict lawyer. I remember well the awful conception of God which I got when I was a boy. I was given an illustrated edition of Watts' hymns, and amongst others there was one hymn which represented God as a great piercing eye in the midst of a great black thunder cloud. The idea of God which that picture gave to my young imagination was of a great detective playing the spy upon my actions; as the hymn says:

"Writing now the story of what little children do."

Such lines as this gave me a bad idea which it has taken me years to obliterate. We think of God as "up there"; there is no such place as "up there." Do not think that God is "up there." You say, God made the world six thousand years ago, and then retired; that is the last that was seen of Him; He made the world and then went to look on, and keep things going. Geology has been away back there, and God has gone farther and farther back; this six thousand years has extended out into ages and ages, and long, long periods. Where is God if He is not "up there" or "back there?," "up there" in space, or "back there" in time—where is He? "The word is nigh thee, even in thy mouth." "The Kingdom of God is within you," and God Himself is among men. When are we to exchange the terrible far away, absentee God of our childhood for the everywhere present God of the Bible? The God of theology has been largely taken from the old Roman Christian writers, who, great as they were, had nothing better to form their conception of God upon than the greatest man. The greatest man to them was the Roman emperor, and therefore God to them became a kind of divine emperor. The Greeks had a far grander conception which is again finding expression in modern theology. The Greek God is the God of this Book; the Spirit which moved upon the waters; the God in whom we live, and move, and have our being; the God of whom Jesus spoke to the women at the well, the God who is a spirit. Let us gather the conception of an imminent God; that is the theological word for it, and it is a splendid word, Immanuel—God with us—an inside God, an imminent God.

Long, long ago, God made matter, then He made the flowers and trees and animals, then He made man. Did He stop? Is God dead? If He lives and acts what is He doing? He is making men better. He is carrying on the development of men. It is God which "worketh in you." The buds of our nature are not all out yet; the sap to make them bloom comes from the

God who made us, from the indwelling Christ. Our bodies are the temples of the Holy Ghost, and we must bear this in mind because the sense of God is kept up not by logic, but by experience,—we must try to keep alive this sense of God.

You have heard of Helen Keller, the Boston girl, who was born deaf, and dumb, and blind; until she was seven years of age her life was an absolute blank; nothing could go into that mind because the ears and eyes were closed to the outer world. Then by that great process which has been discovered, by which the blind see, the deaf hear, and the mute speak, the girl's soul became opened, and they began to put in little bits of knowledge, and bit by bit to educate her. But they reserved the religious instruction for Phillips Brooks. When she was twelve years old they took her to him and he talked to her through the medium of the young lady who had been the means of opening her senses, and who could communicate with her by the exceedingly delicate process of touch. He began to tell her about God, and what He had done, and how He loves men and what He is to us. The child listened very intelligently, and finally said, "Mr. Brooks, I knew all of that before, but I did not know His name." Have you not often felt something within you that was not you, some mysterious pressure, some impulse, some guidance, something lifting you and impelling you to do that which you would not yourself ever have conceived of? Perhaps you did not know His name—"It is God that worketh in you." If we can really found our life upon that great simple fact, the first principle of religion, which we are so apt to forget, that God is with us and in us, we will have no difficulty or fear about our future life.

Two Americans who were crossing the Atlantic, met in the cabin on Sunday night to sing hymns. As they sang the last hymn, "Jesus lover of my soul," one of them heard an exceedingly rich and beautiful voice behind him. He looked around and although he did not know the face, he thought that he knew the voice, so when the music ceased, he turned around and asked the man if he had not been in the civil war. The man replied that he had been a confederate soldier. "Were you at such a place on such a night?" asked the first. "Yes," he replied, "and a curious thing happened that night which this hymn has recalled to my mind. I was posted on sentry duty in the edge of a wood. It was a dark night and very cold and I was a little frightened because the enemy were supposed to be very near. About midnight when everything was very still and I was feeling homesick and miserable and weary, I thought that I would comfort myself by praying and singing a hymn. I remember singing this hymn,

"'All my trust on Thee is stayed,
All my help from Thee I bring
Cover my defenceless head
With the shadow of Thy wing."

After singing that a strange peace came down upon me, and through the long night I remember having felt no more fear."

"Now," said the other, "Listen to my story. I was a Union soldier and was in the wood that night with a party of scouts. I saw you standing, although I did not see your face. My men had their rifles focused upon you, waiting the word to fire, but when you sang out,

"'Cover my defenceless head
With the shadow of Thy wing,'

I said, 'Boys, lower your rifles, we will go home.'"

God was working in each of them. By just such means, by His every where acting mysterious Spirit, God keeps His people and guides them, and hence that second great element in life, God; without Him life is but a living death.

The third element in life about which I wish to speak is Love. The first is Work, the second is God, and the third is Love. In this picture you notice the delicate sense of companionship brought out by the young man and the young woman. It matters not whether they are brother and sister, or lover and loved, there you have the idea of friendship, the final ingredient in our life, after the two I have named. If the man or the woman had been standing in that field alone it would have been incomplete. Love is the divine element in life, because "God is love," and because "he that loveth is born of God"; therefore, as one has said, let us "keep our friendships in repair." They are worth while spending time over, because they constitute so large a part of our life. Let us cultivate this spirit of friendship that it may grow into a great love, not only for our friends but for all humanity. Those of you who are going to the mission field must remember that your mission will be a failure unless you cultivate this element.

So these three things complete life. Some of us may not have these ingredients in their right proportion, but if our life is not comfortable, if we are incomplete, let us ascertain if we are not lacking in one or the other of these three things, and then let us pray for it and work for it.

The Ideal Man

You are to have many speakers tonight, and my words are necessarily exceedingly few, and I desire to devote them however informal they may be, to state principles; because when one gets hold of principles, one can arrange many facts and many ideas and many aspirations around them. And I want to be quite informal—this is an informal night, it is the last night we shall be together, and we talk to one another with more intimacy perhaps than we would be apt to do on a platform night.

I started out some years ago, when I was a student, to find out the meaning of life, to discover what was the ideal-life, and I went for my information to this Book, where I found a sketch of an ideal man, which I want to give you in a very few words, in the language of this book.

The definition of the ideal man I found to be this; "A man after my own heart who shall fulfil all my will."

The first thing a man needs is a reason for being born at all. What are we here for? What is the object of life? I found this answer to that question: "I come to do thy will, O God." And that is the principle which a Christian life ought to be built upon. Our Christian experience is very apt to be made of scraps, bits of sermons, stray texts, and isolated sentences instead of being of a piece and of increasing forces directed constantly from the beginning of life until the curtain drops. If we realized that we come into the world to do the will of God and set the helm steady from the beginning, our lives would work out to a great purpose. The real object of life is simply to do the will of God. When Mr. Moody was in London some years ago, they put up for his meetings, a building which held ten thousand people. After the meetings were over, this building which was put up at a great cost was to be taken down. A number of the committee said, "Well, it is rather a shame to take down this great house after only a few months' use; could we not get some of the great preachers to preach to the people? "They wrote to Mr. Spurgeon, and asked him to come there for a week. They said, "Here is a chance to reach ten thousand people every night," and they magnified the part Mr. Spurgeon would have to these vast crowds. Mr. Spurgeon wrote a letter back to Mr. Moody which I happened to see, and it began with these words, "I have no ambition to preach to ten thousand people, but to do the will of God;" and he declined. The responsibility lay with him to satisfy his own conscience as to why he declined, but what struck me about that letter was that it exposed the vertebral column of that great Christian life. "I have no ambition to do this or to do that, but to do the will of God."

The first thing a baby needs who comes into the world and begins to live is food. I searched my Bible for food for the ideal man, and I found it: "My meat is to do the will of Him who sent me."

After a child has food, the next thing needed is companionship. The hunger of the affections begins to speak, and the child begins to feel around after objects of affection. Hence, the next thing the ideal man needs is friends; and I started out to see what company he would have, and I found this: "Whosoever doeth the will of my Father which is in heaven, the same is my mother, and sister and brother." All the people in the world, black and white, rich and poor, educated and illiterate, who are doing the will of God, are my mother, my brother, and my sister. They may not believe as I believe; they may not hold the same form of church government as I hold; that doesn't disinherit them, or dismember them from the family. "Whosoever doeth the will of God, the same is my mother and sister and brother."

The next thing an ideal man wants, after he has his friends, is language. Although I cannot find any kind of language he is to talk to his earthly friends, yet I can learn a great deal what it ought to be from the ideal man's prayers, the language which he uses in talking to his Father: "Thy will be done." And let us notice that this prayer does not mean resignation; it is not passive, but active.

To pray this prayer is not in effect to say, "God evidently is going to have his way and we may just as well succumb; it is of no use to kick against the pricks; let us just resign at once; Thy will be done." It is an active prayer, and means, "Let that will work through the earth; let it be done in the world; let it be as energetic in the world, as it is triumphant in heaven, until it carries and sweeps everything in the earth along with it!" "Thy will be done!"

All men may be saved; hence the prayer Thy will be done is followed by the expression, "Thy kingdom come."

It is the will of God that Christ's program for the world should be carried out, and the ideal man will turn away from all the other objects and ambitions one by one until he has centred himself and gives the last drop of his blood to the coming of Christ's kingdom. The kingdom of God is coming in Northfield about as plain as in any other part of the world, perhaps a great deal plainer. Those who know Northfield to-day, and those who knew it twenty years ago, know that even in that short time the kingdom of Christ has been coming here. Things are possible here now that were impossible then; lives are lived here now that were not then; the whole atmosphere of the place has felt the influence of Christ. If you could pass that on to every town in America and to every city, we should see, even in our own lifetime, the kingdom of God coming; and it should be our business, if we try to lead the ideal life, to have God's will done in our town and in our state and city as it is clone in heaven. Let us localize that prayer; let us localize it and particularize it and get it into the bit of the world that we are responsible for and not lose it in space—"Thy will be done."

I will dwell for a few moments on the other parts of the ideal life. Education is the next thing an ideal man wants: "Teach me to do thy will, O God." One might go on to speak of the enjoyments of the ideal life: "I delight to do thy will, O God; thy statutes have been my song in the house of my pilgrimage." The pleasure of life consists in living along the lines of God's will.

The close of life, the final step of life, the end of it all, is an eternal life; all the other lives may be very fine, beautiful and interesting, and in their way useful, but this is an eternal life,—"He that doeth the will of God abideth forever." Not an hour of a life lived along that line can be lost, because it is a mere conductor to the eternal, a mere physical means of communicating the spiritual law to this natural world. George Eliot says, "I know no failure save failure in cleaving to the purposes which I know to be the best." I fancy we all know pretty well that this is the best purpose to which we can put our life,—to do the will of God, and our lives cannot fail so long as we do that. That principle equalizes all life, it makes a life lived in the kitchen and a life lived in the pulpit equally heroic, equally Christian and equally divine, because a servant girl in the kitchen can do the will of God just as much as Mr. Spurgeon from his platform. When life is all over, nothing greater can be said of any man than that he did the will of God, whatever that was.

I close by giving you a text indirectly connected with this: "Seek first the kingdom of God." Seek it first! It is not worth while being a Christian unless a man makes it his meat and drink to do the will of God, and help on Christ's kingdom; and I dare say many of you have found out a further secret, not only that it is not worth while, but that it is a hundred times easier to seek the kingdom of God first than it is to seek it second. A man is very apt to think that if he gets more religious and more earnest, life will be come more complicated, and everything will be very much more difficult. That is not true. Life becomes vastly more simple and vastly more easy the more that a man determines that he will seek first the kingdom of God. Just in proportion as we link our wills with the will of God, there will be a lasting outcome from our lives. Some years ago the Atlantic cable was broken, and the operator on the coast of Ireland used to stay at night and watch the needle, as it waved back and forth trying to utter itself in inarticulate words. For months and months this incoherent muttering went on without any meaning, but one night as he watched the needle, he thought he noticed a change, and he tried to follow what it was saying. He saw it spell out a coherent syllable, and that was followed by a second syllable and a third, and a fourth, until he read whole sentences. In mid ocean the cable had been joined. You know an incoherent, inarticulate muttering comes from a man's voice, or lips, or life, who is not linked with the will of God. The moment those two wills touch and are joined together, and keep together, life begins to spell out its great words, and the messages from the other side become real and intelligent. It is only as we can keep up this connection and live habitually in this great stream of existence in the will of God, which is the winning force in life, that our lives can count for Him.

www.ingramcontent.com/pod-product-compliance
Lightning Source LLC
Chambersburg PA
CBHW031659040426
42453CB00006B/343